C0-ANA-921

A Letter from Lisieux

A Letter from Lisieux

Agnès de Jésus, Mother

The Biography of one Sister of
Saint Therese of Lisieux written
by another of her Sisters while
Hitler made war on France.

101,719

Translation and Commentary by
John Mathias Haffert

The Scapular Press : Sea Isle City, N. J.

1942

Nihil Obstat

JACOBUS BULFIN
Censor Deputatus

Imprimatur

✠BARTHÓLOMAEUS JOSEPH
Episcopus Camdensis

Contents

Dedicated

to

my sister,

Sister Therese of the Queen of Carmel, O. D. C.

MAIN CHARACTERS

SISTER MARY OF THE SACRED HEART
formerly Marie Louise Martin

Her Parents
Mr. Louis Stanislaus Martin
Mrs. Zélie (Guérin) Martin

Her Sisters

(*Name in the world*)	(*Name in religion*)
PAULINE (*Writer of the letter*)	Mother Agnes of Jesus
Céline	Sr. Genevieve of the Holy Face
Léonie	Sr. Frances Teresa
THERESE (*Canonized*)	Sr. Therese of the Child Jesus

Other Characters

His Holiness, Pope Pius XII

Père Pichon, S. J., Confessor of Sr. Mary of the Sacred Heart

Louise, maid in the Martin household

The Chaplain, aide at Sister Mary's death

The Story of This Book

On February 27, 1940, the eldest sister of Saint Therese of Lisieux passed to her eternal reward.

To many, even in 1942, this will be "news".

Perhaps future generations will look upon it as "significant".

It was this sister with whom Saint Therese shared one of the biggest trials of her life—the trial of scruples. It was this sister who stood for the Saint in Baptism as Godmother. It was this sister who knelt at the Saint's bedside, during the latter's almost mortal childhood illness, and stormed Heaven for the miracle we know as "The Virgin's Smile"—the miracle of a statue animated at the Saint's bedside. It was this sister who looked on Therese as a Saint—and caused the writing of the famous "Story of a Soul", the Saint's Autobiography. Yes, it was this sister—the sister convinced that Therese's sanctity was a Way of Life for us of the twentieth century—who left this world at our century's darkest hour.

A Letter From Lisieux

I learned about the death of "Marie"—known in religion as "Soeur Marie du Sacré Coeur"—when, visiting at a monastery of Carmelite nuns, the sisters had asked me to translate a letter they had just received from Lisieux—a letter telling the story of "Marie".

It was well over two years ago, but it might have been yesterday. From the first page, I typed furiously. In the atmosphere that seemed to sweep over the monastery walls into the room of the adjoining guest house, every line was doubly significant.

At some lines, I smiled; at others, tears shone at the corners of my eyes. Again and again I exclaimed at the spiritual beauty of that message—a message that came while Europe was embroiled in a horible war.

During the past two years, I was frequently back at that table in the monastery guest house, particularly after Hitler, sweeping right over Lisieux, successfully invaded France; I relived my emotions and the thought occurred and reoccurred that certainly others would like to read that Letter from Lisieux.

But consideration of one problem gave me pause.

I thought: "Even if American Catholics do read the Letter from Lisieux, most will probably be moved, say it is profound and masterful, but miss the secret of this letter even as so many missed the secret of the Little Flower's Autobiography. And if I essay to analyze the secret, it may not be taken well."

The secret is Affiliation to the Blessed Virgin, particularly through the devotion of the Holy Scapular to which Our Lady attached a Promise of Salvation.

I wondered why the Scapular was not mentioned in the Letter from Lisieux. "Marie" was a Carmelite, and she had set an example of Scapular sanctity as Therese had done.

Yes, she had done more.

She had lived the Little Way for almost a century, and therefore leaving a message consequently as important as the message left by Saint Therese— as readers of the Letter from Lisieux will see for themselves.

I had decided to do the book anyway when this doubt, that for a time prevented its completion, was suddenly solved in a very dramatic, though somewhat sad, manner.

Mother Mary Teresa, the Carmelite Prioress and foundress of the Carmel at Schenectady, N. Y., had given me permission to translate her copy of the Letter from Lisieux when she died suddenly and unexpectedly on March nineteenth of this year—only a few weeks after sending me the letter to be translated for publication.

Mother Teresa had a great reputation for sanctity, and a large number of friends. A few weeks after her death I received a little booklet written about her—almost identical in purpose to the Letter from Lisieux—together with a personal letter from the succeeding Prioress that read:

"Many indeed are the sweet memories which we treasure of our dearest Mother, but it would be impossible to include them all in such a brief sketch as this. You yourself can easily guess what a love she had for Our Lady's holy Scapular, and the zeal with which she endeavored to propagate the devotion by printed leaflets and pamphlets, distributing gratis as many of your grand books as holy poverty permitted, both among priests, religious, and lay persons, and

persuading the families of each of our Sisters to secure a copy. She would urge us to make numbers of Scapulars to distribute, and encouraged our relatives, as well as the friends and benefactors of the community, to hang them in their homes to obtain our Lady's protection during these dangerous times. Often and often she would remark, as she plied her needle in the making of a scapular: 'We do not know what soul may wear this scapular. Some soul may die in this and it will be the means of saving it.' But it was above all in her last illness that our dear Mother showed how persevering was her zeal in this regard. She had worn herself out many years before her time by her arduous labors in the service of God, and in those last months, due to the extremely weakened condition of her heart, her sight was dimmed. With trembling hands she would try to sew scapulars, but what a supreme effort it cost her in this condition! She would work at this loved task until her dear hands would drop in her lap.

"On the very morning of the day she died, March nineteenth, we had made quite a number of scapulars as a little feast day gift, and had placed them on a small table at the feet of a statue of our

Father St. Joseph. As there were too many to lay at his feet, we had hung a number of them about his neck. We placed the table in front of Mother when she went to our improvised infirmary for her morning meal. She always had a sense of humor and said to the Infirmarian with a sweet smile: 'Our Father St. Joseph is going to save HIS soul.' Sister answered: 'Yes, and also all the souls entrusted to Him, too.' How little we knew our dear Mother would die that night!"

To my astonishment, although I learned, through this personal letter, that the Scapular was paramount in Mother Teresa's life, I could not find one mention of the Scapular in the entire booklet that told her life-story!

And I realized that probably had a lay person written Mother Teresa's story, the Scapular would certainly have been mentioned. But the Scapular is so close to the Carmelites—so usual and so taken for granted—that they would not think of mentioning it in a story that is supposed to touch only salient points in a life time.

Affiliation to Mary is not salient to them because it is their life entirely.

The Story of This Book

So "A Letter from Lisieux" is being published —including an explanatory chapter on the Scapular. And while it is being published another book is being mailed to all Carmels about Mother Teresa just as this Letter from Lisieux, which was as moving and as dear to her as it was to us, came from France two years before.

Certainly, from Heaven, Mother Teresa will pray for every one of the readers of "A Letter from Lisieux"—pray that this message of peace and of the Little Way, in this time of world conflict, will find its way deep into all our hearts.

JOHN MATHIAS HAFFERT.

August 13, 1942.

A Letter from Lisieux

"The road lies clear, and perforce do we run
it together. I feel that Jesus wishes to bestow
on us both a free entrance into His Kingdom."

Words addressed to her sister Mary by
SAINT THERESE OF THE CHILD JESUS

Chapter One

February 27, 1940

On February 27, 1940, after Hitler's troops had stormed into Poland, with dive-bomber and tank, and were now skirmishing at the Maginot line to bring the horrible blitzkrieg into France, this biographical letter was written in a small town in northern France where a nun had died.

Copies went to Carmelite Convents, in the four corners of the world, where they were read with tenderness and tears.

It is a human document.

The nun who had passed away, the eldest sister of Saint Therese of Lisieux, known in religion as Sister Mary of the Sacred Heart, was not dead. She had merely left her convent to invade the world far more thoroughly and quite differently than Nazi troops. She had started anew her life of doing good on earth, as her sister had done little more than forty years previously when she, too, set out, saying: *"I will spend my Heaven doing good upon earth."*

19

Most people would say that the greatest point of interest in the life of this recently deceased nun is her nearness to Saint Therese, who became Patroness of Catholic Missions, Star of the Pontificate of the great Pontiff, Pius XI, and whose statues are to be found in thousands upon thousands of churches, in every corner and cranny of the world.

But others will say that she has her own claim to fame.

She was an astonishing soul, simple and very human; passionate for freedom . . . yet happy under the fetters of vows; independent . . . yet lost without someone on whom to depend; saintly . . . yet quite different from her sainted sister.

It is to this nun that we owe the existence of the book "The Story of a Soul," the Autobiography of Saint Therese of Lisieux, which has done more to change the world, in more parts of the world, than perhaps any other book written in the last half-century.

And she has a master biographer in Mother Agnes of Jesus . . . Prioress of the community at Lisieux . . . who wrote this present, famous letter. We seldom get a biography that draws aside the veil and shows the soul. But here is a poignant writing that lifts the veil. It really seems like a continuation of the autobiography of Saint Therese.

Men are followers. Even leaders, in a sense, follow those whom they lead. And there is one quality which all mankind acknowledges and instinctively follows . . . the quality of self-sacrifice, motivated by love.

Saint Therese of Lisieux had this quality. That is why she was able to cross, not the boundaries of nations but, the boundaries of millions of human hearts; to cross and to conquer for her Sovereign.

And while one of the bloodiest wars in the entire History of the World was about to embrace Lisieux in a mad whirl that would end in the thunder of Dunkerque, a living sister of Saint Therese wrote this masterpiece over the hardly cold remains of the Saint's eldest sister, who was known in the world as "Mary" (*Marie*) and in religion as "Sister Mary of the Sacred Heart" (*Soeur Marie du Sacré Coeur*). This eldest sister of Saint Therese, also a leader, had set forth from a war-torn world to frank the boundaries of human hearts . . . with a message of "the little way" she had herself fulfilled.

When one reads the story of this newly famed recluse of Lisieux . . . the recluse who left her solitude in our century's darkest hour . . . one is aware that he is reading of a person quite different from Saint Therese, yet who understood no mystery of sanctity other than "the little way" . . . who had much to do with tiny sacrifices, the beauty of a setting sun, the sadness of separation, the exhilaration of great and little successes, and the ever joyous job of loving God . . . to the point of heroism.

The writer who draws aside the veil from this beautiful and different soul is the celebrated Mother Agnes of Jesus, who was known in the world as "Pauline". She is the one whom both Saint Therese and Sister Mary tenderly called not only their sister but their "little Mother". This fact, as the reader will see, contributes immensely to the significance and tenderness of this Letter from Lisieux, which Mother Agnes wrote as a death-announcement to the Prioresses of other Carmelite convents.

Having read it, one would not be ashamed to say that more than once it drew a tear, of joy or of sympathy.

"You ask for a word from me," Saint Therese once wrote to Sister Mary of the Sacred Heart, "but what shall I say? Is it not *you* who taught me? Remember those days when I sat on your knee and you talked to me of Paradise?"

The story closes with a two-word description of Sister Mary . . . two words packed with drama and meaning:

"She knows!"

What does she know . . . this other recluse of Lisieux? Or what, even, *did* she know? As she lay on her death-bed, did she know that in a few months France would be conquered? Did she know that Poland, Catholic Poland, buffer between Nazi Germany and Communist Russia, had been over-run, Warsaw was in flames, and the blood of millions already spilled in a war that would soon embrace almost every nation of the world? Did she know that the great British Empire was being hacked away in every corner of the globe? Did she know that America was to be attacked as a continent of "United Nations," and that Hitler aimed at a unified Europe, Nazi-controlled and paganized?

What *does* she know?

Chapter Two

Free

(The Letter Opens . . . Mother Agnes Writing)

Peace, and greetings in Our Lord Who called to Himself, on January the nineteenth of the Jubilee Year of the profession of Saint Therese of the Child Jesus, the eldest sister and god-mother of Saint Therese, our very dear SISTER LOUISE JOSE-PHINE MARY of the SACRED HEART, the Senior Professed of our Community. She was eighty years of age, less one month, and had passed fifty-three years, three months and three days in religion.

Our dear Sister was born at Alençon on February 22, 1860. It is very delicate for us to eulogize her pious parents, who are also our own parents and whom you know further through the Autobiography of Saint Therese. However, as we have been asked to have no fear in the course of this letter to evoke, for the interest of the narration, memories which we may have in common with our well-beloved Sister, in all simplicity shall we do so.

From childhood, Mary showed herself to be a

judicious observer, full of originality, and tended to independence.

The maid, Louise, who was very authoritative, terrorized us if we dared to resist her in anything. She tried to gather Mary under her rigorous tute-lage, too, but to each rude injunction Mary answered fearlessly: "Leave me be, Louise, I'm quite free!" So the servant surnamed her: *I'm quite free!*

Some notes, letters written to us on our express command, because Mary did not like to put her thoughts into writing, will aid us in this narration. She writes:

"When I was taken to Mass and heard the little bell sound at the Elevation, on seeing everyone immediately bow his head I said to myself: 'It is too much to force us to bow our heads like that, it pleases me better to look; I am quite free!' And, indeed, I looked; I still see the white Host in the hands of the priest. But finally I understood why all the foreheads were lowered. The first time I contemplated the Sacred Host while making my act of independence, I felt an impression of sweet-ness and peace.

"Besides, I never wanted to bow to persons whom we knew. It humiliated me to make a bow. I remember that one day I deliberately turned my head away like a little savage. Mother was pained to see that I had such a singular character and she told me that no one would love me. But this only added fuel to the fire of my haughty spirit. Thinking that one had to be polite and make bows in order to be loved, I said to myself: 'It displeases me to try to make others love me. No, I won't subject myself to that!' And I said to mother: 'It's all right with me if people do not love me; if you love me, that's enough.' "

Then she narrates her first sacrifice:

"You want me, Mother, to put my first act of virtue in writing. Here it is:

"I was about four or five years old. You remember that Papa had, on a little table in his store, a dried orange skin in which he put pennies. I thought that was so marvellous that one day, when I was given an orange, I asked him to make a little saucer for me, just like his, and then, completely triumphant, I showed it to you. At once it made you envious and, *to have a pearl in my crown* (that was the way mother used to make us do things) I gave it to you. It seemed to me that I was accomplishing an heroic act, because that famous orange skin seemed all the more precious to me because you wanted it. Then, running quickly towards mother, I said: 'Mama, I gave my orange skin to Pauline. Will I go to Heaven?' Mother smiled and answered: 'Yes, my little daughter, you will go to Heaven.' That hope alone was able to console me for the loss of *my fortune*.

"Alas, Mother, while thinking today of this little act of my childhood I find that most of the time we hardly have more than little acts to offer the good God. One meets great sacrifices rarely, but the very little ones, the little dried orange peels, one obtains in as great abundance as one could wish. Thus, at this moment, I have only to give my little *yellow saucer* and I am sure, very sure, that Jesus will place therein not pennies, but diamonds for Paradise . . . SOULS. And do you know what my little orange peel is at the moment? Well, it is the house that is being built behind the trees and great wall, just opposite our cell. All the country that I used to love to see is going to disappear before my eyes; already I no longer see the little white houses with windows sparkling in the evening to the touch of the setting sun. That used to make me think of Heaven. I used to say to myself that, in Heaven, it is thus that the Blessed must reflect together the Divine Sun, and that the most simple souls, too, will shine like suns. I have therefore offered this little sacrifice with all those that Jesus accomplished for poor sinners, in order that the fearful wall of His Justice may never rise before them to hide from them, forever, their Sovereign Good. O! when one thinks of that irreparable unhappiness! How I would like to save souls! For that it is necessary to be holy, for it is only the saints who are powerful in appeasing His Justice. Finally, I am His spouse, and His love for me blinds Him perhaps . . . ?"

Let us now return to the first years of our dear Sister's life . . . but how many times will we have to speak of her zeal for souls, which she manifested towards all until death!

She was eight and a half years old when she was put to board with us at the Visitation of Mans, where our maternal aunt, Sister Mary Dosithea was.* Never, as we shall see, did Sister Mary of the Sacred Heart entirely accustom herself to this separation from the family.

Her First Communion was advanced a year because our aunt fell gravely ill, and we wanted to

---

* The parents of the Martin sisters were models. It is little wonder that all the Martin girls loved both parents with an almost fathomless love. Mrs. Martin, before meeting Louis Martin (in the Church of Our Lady, at Alençon, just before the Feast of Our Lady of the Scapular, in 1858) had her heart set on joining the Sisters of Charity but had been counselled to remain in the world. Her only sister entered the Convent of the Visitation at Le Mans, taking the name Sister Mary Dosithea, and was undoubtedly as admirable and holy as Mrs. Martin. Dom Guéranger, author of *The Liturgical Year* and probably the most outstanding Benedictine of the nineteenth century, cites Sister Dosithea as the model of a perfect nun. [Ed.]

give Sister Dosithea this consolation before death. The first Mistress of the boarding house had therefore informed Mary that, if she was very learned, she would make her First Communion when she was nine years old. This hope gave Mary courage and she learned her Catechism with extraordinary ardor. It was a feast for her to go and recite her lesson to the chaplain of the Monastery. When the chaplain asked questions that the others could not answer, she thought: "O! How I wish he'd ask me! I know it so well!"

That is exactly what happened very often, and the venerable priest might have called her, too, as he did Saint Therese, his *"little doctor."*

Besides this ardent study, Mary made many little sacrifices to prepare herself well for the reception of the good Jesus.

She writes:

"In the intimacy of my soul, I used to think that Our Lord had made everyone think that my aunt was going to die just because He was anxious to give Himself to me. This thought filled me with joy."

However, we were told repeatedly that our aunt could not recover without a miracle, but little Mary preserved an unshakable faith.

One day, when the two of us had gone to see Sister Mary Dosithea in the infirmary when she was so oppressed that she could scarcely talk, the infirmarian tried to make Mary understand that, above all, it was necessary to be abandoned to the Will of God. Then Mary looked at her, stupefied, and said:

"But, Sister, if I acted like that, I would get nowhere. If, by misfortune, it were not God's Will that my aunt be cured, I would be sure my prayers would not be heard; I guard myself carefully against talking to Him of His Will, but I try to change His Will." The good sister smiled at this strange theology and did not know what to say in answer . . .

She also addressed herself to Saint Joseph with a naive and tenacious confidence. If she met a religious while going to the chapel, after asking "How is my aunt?", on receiving the answer she cast a glance at the statue of Saint Joseph, either to scold him or to thank him, and never doubting about the miracle.

She was heard and, in recognition to the good Saint Joseph, she took the name *Josephine* at her Confirmation. The pious aunt could then assist, cured, at the First Communion of her fervent niece.

Chapter Three

More Orange Peels

What a good First Communion our little Mary made! She was like an angel, and so well prepared! She was happy, too, because she was chosen to recite the act of faith which so well summed up the sentiments of her soul. But in the evening, before going to sleep, she was heard sobbing, dissolved in tears. To the Mistress, who ran to learn the cause of her sorrow, she answered through her sobs: "It is because the day of my First Communion is over!"

"The next day," we read in her intimate notes, "we were returned to our parents. Ah! That day! How melancholy it was to me! I had refound father and mother . . . I who had suffered so much in being separated from them. With them I seemed to be in Heaven, but that Heaven had to be very short because, that very evening, they had to leave us! Besides, my happiness was far from complete. We took a walk in the country and soon I saw a field filled with daisies and cornflowers, but to pick them I would have had to leave go Papa's hand, and I preferred to remain beside him. I looked at him,

I looked at mother . . . There was, in my little heart of nine years, an abyss of tenderness for them.

"It would be impossible for me to say how much I suffered in being separated from my parents. It would be in vain that I should try to explain that martyrdom. Ah! If it were not that I had an aunt whom I could never have caused the least pain, I would never have remained seven years behind a grille, because then I did not have the vocation to live behind grilles . . . I had not yet heard the call of Jesus, that call which renders sweet that which is bitter to nature. Did He not say Himself: *'No one comes to me, except My Father draw him . . .* '? Now that He has drawn me I find myself, behind grilles, the happiest of creatures. I find myself in possession of true liberty. Ah! It is now that I can really say: *'I am quite free!'* "

Our aunt, who alone could keep Mary boarding at the Visitation, loved her particularly because of her directness, her extraordinary frankness. The child would run to her ceaselessly to accuse herself. "Aunty, I again lost time at the beginning of study, I have done this and that . . . " Sister Mary Dosithea was ravished by such a disposition, but nevertheless she sometimes found her little niece very original. One day, among others, that Sister Dosithea sent Mary to put some flowers on an altar of Our Lady of the Seven Dolors, this reflection burst forth: "Aunty, why in the world does one put bouquets before the saints, backwards? One ought to turn the flowers towards them. This way your Blessed Virgin sees nothing but iron wires!"

"My little daughter," answered her aunt, "do you put your dress on backwards to have the beautiful side towards you?" The child was quiet. She had understood.

"At the ages of eleven and twelve," she relates, "I gave more trouble to my aunt who was, until then, very satisfied with me. When I came to say, for example (always accusing myself): 'Aunty, I find that there are many repetitions of words in the Gospel; our Mistress of style teaches us, however, to avoid repetitions,' she took on a severe air and, almost indignant, said to me: 'Go now, and try to find further fault with the words of Our Lord!' And I, completely confused at such a thought while confiding it to her, said to myself interiorly: 'Well! I won't begin again to tell her such ideas, since she makes such an affair of it!' "

A religious, thinking to give her pleasure, said: "Your sister Pauline is very genteel." And she immediately came back with: "That's true, Sister, but the others are genteel, too." Sister Dosithea was informed of this and scolded her. "But, Aunty, I don't understand," she said. "I love Pauline so much that when someone compliments her in my presence I feel that the compliments are also addressed to me, and I thought I had to answer the way I did."

Mary was a very good student and succeeded perfectly in her studies. She won numerous prizes, and they were well merited because, at the Visitation, only a few prizes were given, sometimes only one.

Each tri-semester, she was the one who most often obtained the Cross of Excellence, had her name on the List of Honor, and received "decorations," that is, large ribbons of different colors with gold or silver borders. There was the ribbon of Christian Doctrine (white), the ribbon of Honor (blue), the ribbon of Diligence (violet). And, at the services on Sunday, the favored students wore these ribbons across their breasts.

Once when the first Mistress was putting one of these ribbons on Mary she whispered to her: "Through favor!" Then Mary did not want to wear it, not through spite, but really, as she said, "Because I do not want to adorn myself with something that is unmerited."

She was nearing her thirteenth birthday when, during the Christmas vacations, the good God sent us our "Little Therese." On the morning of January 2nd, 1873, Mary approached the cradle with a bliss mixed with respect. "Embrace your little sister," Mother said to her. The day after next, with more assurance, she became the happy godmother* . . . a sweet and happy and glorious memory to follow her and be a grace to her all her life.

That year she was attacked with typhoid fever and had to leave the boarding-school. On one of his visits, the doctor said to our parents: "This child must have been broken hearted, it is rather a bilious fever than typhoid fever that she suffers . . ." The little invalid heard and said in a whisper: "That is indeed true!" and she was comforted to think that now they had proof of what she had suffered in being separated from her loved ones.

When she was cured, our good mother very seriously suggested that she give up her studies at Alençon. But Mary refused, manifesting that self-sacrifice that was truly her dominant quality: "No, Mama, that would cause Aunty too much pain. I prefer to return to the Visitation."

---

* "Godmother" means "Responsible Representative of the soul in the vows of Baptism," and to have been such a representative for a Saint was a signal blessing and honor. [Ed.]

Chapter Four

Human

On her return to the school this time, Mary found a pupil of her own age, pious and charming, who awakened the deepest of her sympathetic feelings. She loved her and was loved in return. But, little by little, this affection preoccupied her so much that she lost the beautiful liberty of her heart. She desired to be noble and rich like her friend, she desired to know the world—the vanities of which, however, she already knew well.

Soon she was not lacking in little pettinesses, "Bewitchment of baubles which seduce even the soul distant from evil." She was proud of being brought up at the Visitation, where most of her companions belonged to the nobility, and she did not deprive herself of the pleasure of boasting of their beautiful estates.

At the end of the summer vacation, one year, when Mary was walking with our good father in a modest family property, named Roulée, she began to pick some flowers, saying: "I am going to take these flowers to the Visitation as a memory of

36

Roulée." And Papa answered archly: "That's it! And then you will put on airs with your friends, showing them flowers from your estate." Then, very vexed at finding herself devined, Mary briskly tossed her bouquet into the grass.

But let us return to that exaggerated affection which inspired the following reflections in her:

"Alas! that instead of my foolish dreams of creatures I have not flown straight to Thee, like my little Therese, O my God! Thou dost also dream of the creature . . . but Thou dost not dream as we do . . . Thou dost consider the creature to divinize it. Sometimes, O mystery!, thou dost consider the creature to make it Thy spouse! And it is this dream of love that is realized in me!"

Eleven years later, on the point of entering Carmel, she saw her friend a second time who, after some waverings about a religious vocation, had taken another road. Mary had difficulty recognizing her. "All her beauty," she confides to us, "had withered like the flower of the field. For myself, I resolved to fly finally towards the unique Beauty Which does not pass. My dreams of nobility and grandeur had passed . . . "

Mary left school when she was fifteen and a half years old. She was a tall and beautiful girl, pure as a lily, with purity she would never alter . . . but she was quite resolved to enjoy all her lib-

erty. Our aunt advised her to say, daily, the prayer
to Saint Joseph, "O Father and Protector of Virgins" but, having read on the fly-leaf: "Special
Prayer for Priests and Religious," she said. "So!
my aunt wants me to be a religious! . . . There is
little danger that I'll say *that* prayer!"

Once by chance, however, when Mary was not
quite sixteen, our mother spoke to her about marriage as a vocation. At the very word 'marriage,'
she broke into tears declaring that she would never
marry, and begged that no one would ever broach
the subject to her.

"Nor did I feel any attraction to self-beautifi-
cation," she tells us, "but in this despising of coquet-
terie there must have been some secret pride because pride slips in everywhere, even in what seems
to be humility. When I put on a new dress, it was
a genuine suffering for me. I especially detested the
little veils of white net which signified nothing because they did not hide the face. When I wore one
I felt as though I were trying to be a beauty! The
day of Léonie's first communion, rigged out in one
of these veils on the way out of the Church, I met
the stylist who had made my hat. She thought I
was sick, so crimson was I under that famous veil,
which was bound to make my complexion dull, and
I was delivered from this *mask à la mode*, as I
called it."

To give her further displeasure, there was the fashion of wearing a medallion sewed into a velvet ribbon that was knotted about the neck. "I thought I looked like a little parlor dog," she used to say, "when I had that velvet around my neck."

It was doubtlessly in just such a circumstance as this that our mother wrote to her sister-in-law, Madame Guérin, at Lisieux: "Mary is a little unsociable and too timid; she has some peculiar ideas. One day when she put on a new outfit, didn't she go into the garden to cry, saying that she was being dressed like a girl whom one desired to marry off at any cost!"

Mary was therefore very serious. Her only pleasure was to occupy herself with her little sisters, especially with Léonie, who, in a religious way, owes her much. Léonie could not accustom herself to the Visitation and took lessons in town. Therese, the youngest, took account of the authority given in the house to the eldest sister. One day when she was in the garden admiring roses that Mary cultivated, mother was getting ready to pluck one and Therese cried out: *"Mama, the roses belong to Mary!"*

Mary consecrated herself entirely to the instruction of Céline.

"Had I had twenty pupils," she declares, "I would not have given myself more trouble. And Therese, who was scarcely three years old, wanted to follow Céline and assist at the lessons. For fear of being chased, she did not budge and never said a word. What a cherub she was! What sweetness! Some authors have wished to give her a different character that they might thus emphasize her virtue of forcefulness, but one must tell only the truth."

Moreover, at the Process she affirmed under oath:

"Sister Therese of the Infant Jesus appeared to me, from her most tender infancy, as though she had been sanctified from her mother's womb, or rather, like an angel whom the Good God had sent to earth in a mortal body. What she calls her imperfections or faults were not such. I never saw her commit the slightest fault."

This testimony of Sister Mary of the Sacred Heart, so precious and formal, corresponds to this period in her life.

She went to Mass every morning at this time, but one could hardly accuse her of over-manifesting her fervor, however profound. This was so true that our mother, not finding her pious enough, used to write to Mans, to Sister Mary Dosithea, and the latter would then address to her niece what she called "Sermons of Sanctity" which, she avows with disarming simplicity, "never had much effect on me."

"Mama," she said one day, "I assure you that I love the good God very much, even more than you think . . . Thus, I love to look at the Tabernacle. It is not worth while to have my lips move. I prefer to hide my feelings."

A year after leaving school, she returned to the Visitation to make a retreat, preached to the graduates by a Jesuit Father. Our devoted aunt then counselled her to open herself to the preacher concerning her vocation and, to content Sister Dosithea, she said to this priest that she had come to him that she might know her vocation, and would he please unveil it to her so there would be no further question about it!"

"But I did not even think of my vocation," she confided later, "I did not have any." Finally I made the best of it, asking this good religious to take me under his direction. He gave me his address. I was sincere, yet quite decided never to write to him.

"Behold the result of my retreat!"

Fundamentally our good aunt and dear mother were not mistaken. They had a secret presentiment of Mary's divine call, as this passage from one of our mother's letters of this time reveals: "I am quite satisfied with Mary," she writes. "The things of this world do not penetrate her heart as deeply as do spiritual things; she is becoming very pious.

41

I believe that she will be a religious; I would like her to be a saint . . . "

It was from Heaven that mother and aunt were to bring this vocation to flower after holy death, which arrived for Sister Dosithea on February 24th, 1877, and for our own dear mother on August 28th of the same year. Mary was seventeen and a half years old.

Chapter Five

Called

Two months after our mother died, in November of 1877, the family left for Lisieux and took up its residence in Buissonets. What forgetfulness of herself and what self-abnegation was revealed by Mary, eldest daughter and sister, in her endeavor to soften the heart-break of her poor father and sisters!

We believe that she received this strength of soul near the mortal remains of our mother, after an entire night passed in tears. While contemplating them, so beautiful and calm in death, she had suddenly experienced *a profound feeling, an assurance that this dear mother was only apparently dead; that she was more living than ever and that she would aid her in all the difficulties of her life.*

Five years later there was a new separation: the separation imposed upon her by the entrance of "her Pauline" into Carmel, and a separation which she again accepted so generously!* Then, six months

---

* "Her Pauline" is Mother Agnes who, as the reader will remember, is telling the story, and the profound affection of Mary for "her Pauline" is therefore passed over. However, this separation must have been most painful. [Ed.]

had not passed after this departure, when Therese
was seized with the mysterious illness that was suddenly cured by the apparition and smile of the
Blessed Virgin on May 13th, 1883—apparition and
smile which the joyful Saint affirmed to have been
a response to the faith and confidence of Mary.

Is it not permitted to us to think today, fifty-
seven years after this memorable event, that Sister
Mary of the Sacred Heart, dying, and fixing a luminous gaze on that same statue of the Blessed Virgin, obtained through the intercession and thank-
fulness of Therese the same celestial and maternal
smile . . . the beginning of her eternal beatitude?

But, while waiting, how many graces she received, and how many Calvaries she had to scale!

The graces! One of them . . . and a very
great one . . . was to prepare Therese for her First
Communion . . . to have seen her, then, through the
grille of the fervent Benedictines, so recollected and
bathed in tears of love . . .

And we read in her personal notes:

"One day, at Buissonets, Therese asked me to
explain what it meant to love God purely and to
forget oneself. I read in her look an ardent desire
to practice what I would teach her. She was like
a warrior, measuring the battlefield on which she
wished to fight and carry away the victory, the victory of love in conquering souls. Looking at her I

said to myself: What will become of this child? Truly she is not ordinary; a certain mystery of predestination seems to hover over her."

It must also be said that Therese, while listening to Mary as she explained such beautiful things, was taken with the thought that later she was to put in writing:

" . . . It seems to me that all her heart . . . so great, so generous . . . passed into mine. Like the warriors of old who taught their children the art of fighting, thus did she teach me about the combat of life, exciting my ardor and showing me the glorious palm. She told me further about the immortal riches that we can so easily amass each day, about the misfortune of trampling them beneath our feet when we have only, so to say, but to stoop over to gather them.

"How eloquent was this dear sister! I wished that I were not the only one to hear her profound teachings; I believed, in my naïveté, that listening to her the greatest sinners would have been converted and that, leaving their perishable riches right there, would no longer have sought ought but those of Heaven."

Was not the cloister a necessity to such a soul? Here are the intimate pages which she wrote to us in 1909 and 1910, at our instant and sisterly request. It is the net story of her vocation and of her happiness in Carmel.

"I was just twenty-two years old," she writes, "when you told me, beloved Mother, that you wanted to be a Carmelite. We had the same confessor and I perceived very well that you knew how to open your soul while I . . . I was like a block of wood. Besides, what would I have confided about my soul? Your desire to enter Carmel did not awaken any vocation in me; therefore I had nothing to say. However, I suffered very much and I remember that one day, after returning from confession, I began to cry when I found myself alone in my room. Then I opened the Imitation and read these words:

" 'Having taken heart after the storm, reassemble your forces at the sight of My mercies because I am near you, says the Lord, to reestablish all things, not only with measure but with abundance and extra measure.'

"Immediately I felt consoled and mystically I said to you: 'Do you see what I have drawn from the Imitation?' It was a mystery for both of us . . .

"Some days later a person of our acquaintance spoke to us with enthusiasm about a Jesuit Father, the Reverend Father Pichon, who had just preached a retreat near Lisieux. 'He is a Saint,' she said, 'a real saint such as one does not meet. You can see him; he is soon to give a mission at Lisieux.'

"Through curiosity, I went to see *the saint*. I heard his Mass and, not having any sins to confess, I entered his confessional saying to myself: 'Do I have to go to confession or should I tell him the true purpose of my visit?' I halted at the latter thought and said to him: 'Father, I came to you to see *a saint.*' He laughed a little at my simplicity and answered: 'All right, my child! Make your confession.' I made a confession, as usual, and left without speaking to him further. While going out I thought: 'Had I known, I would not have disturbed myself . . . '

"But that evening, an ardent desire to see this good father again took possession of me. How was it to be done? Unfortunately I could not go out alone and I had to confide my project to Victoria, (the maid), that she might accompany me. Finally I surmounted all obstacles and the next day I again assisted at the Mass of the good religious. Then I entered his confessional and said: 'Father, I am coming to you again because I feel irresistibly drawn here. Why, I know not.' He put some questions to me and asked me if I wanted to be a religious. 'No, Father,' I answered. 'Do you want to get married, then?' 'O! no, Father!' 'But what do you want to do, then? be an old

maid?' 'O! surely not!' 'Then . . . ?' He added:
'Just now, I am pressed because I have to get a
train in just a few moments, but in fifteen days I
am coming back to Lisieux to preach a retreat at
the Refuge. You can speak to me there. Write
down for me all your impressions on the religious
life and why you do not want it and, finally, write
all you have thought about your vocation during
these days. For my part, I very much hope to
give you to Jesus . . . '

"I was caught in his nets! nets of kindness! I
returned to Buissonets with a heart that was light
and filled with a secret joy. Jesus had then cast on
me, too, a special glance of love! O! I was far from
tempted to imitate the young man of the Gospel and
to sadly go away from Him!

"On the agreed day, I went to see Father
Pichon with my eight, fully written pages, wherein
I had revealed all the most intimate sentiments of
my heart. Not to influence him, I had been careful
to write only what I had thought at the time of my
last visit. After making my confession, I passed my
manuscript to him through the little grille and stood
up to leave, but he kept me for an hour, reading it
before me and making his reflections there and
then. I can tell you that I passed a bad quarter-
hour.

"But I, who formerly had not wanted a director, had one! And I had chosen him of my own will. Or rather, it was God Who had chosen him for me. He arrived at the moment I was going to lose my dear Pauline. I avow that for me he was an *angel of the Lord*. And he also did good to our beloved father, who received him several times at Buissonets as 'friend and director of the Martin family,' as he happily put it.

"From time to time he wrote some very paternal letters to me, but over-burdened by his correspondence and retreats (he preached more than 900 of them) he sometimes left me quite a long time without an answer. I have written him as many as fourteen letters in succession without receiving a single word!

"In 1884, Father Pichon was called to Canada and, at his departure, only the good God knows how much I suffered. He returned in 1886 and I wanted to go to Calais to meet him. When I asked Papa to make this trip, he answered: 'I could refuse you nothing, Mary.'

"We waited two days at Calais, then at Douvres, but in vain. We had been misinformed.

"But when we returned to Paris, we found Father Pichon! I grumbled bitterly at having been deceived, but Papa answered me like a saint: 'One must not murmur, Mary. The good God has judged that you needed this trial and, for my part, I am happy to have been an instrument to Him in making this trip with you.' Ah! Mother, it was indeed true. The good God wished in that manner to further detach me from things of earth, even from the most innocent joys. Now that I have grown older, I see well that during the early years of my life I was not free of illusions. Because why, O my God, why should I run so distractedly towards the creature, even if it were an angel descended from Heaven?

"Without hesitation, I was then very near to entering Carmel. One day in the parlor, Mother, you had said to me that it was time to think of it. Since I did not feel the attraction of any vocation I answered that I would enter when the good God would tell me to but that, until then, He had not yet sufficiently made know His Will to me. Then you said: 'Don't believe that He will appear to you. You are almost twenty-six years old and you have to make a decision.' 'I will not make a decision,' I answered. 'Since God knows well that I desire to do His Will, He will rather send me a celestial messenger to make it known to me.'

"It was then, my little Mother, that you wrote to Father Pichon. And, some days later, I received a letter in which he asked me the age of Céline,[1] and whether it would soon be possible for me to respond to the call of God. I suspected nothing and was left stupefied. The hour of sacrifice was about to fall upon me; Ah! With what little enthusiasm I saw that hour approaching! It meant saying goodbye to a father whom I loved so much! It meant abandoning my sisters. But I did not hesitate a single moment and I made my great confidence known to father. At such an utterly unexpected disclosure, he gave vent to a deep sigh. There was nothing that could have made him suppose that I wanted to become a religious. He stifled a sob and said brokenly: 'Ah! . . Ah! . . But . . without you! . . ' He could not finish. In order not to further arouse his tenderness, I answered with assurance: 'Céline is big enough to replace me. You'll see, Papa, everything will go all right.' Then he said: 'The good God could not have asked a greater sacrifice of me! I thought that you would never leave me!' And he embraced me to hide his emotion . . . I am crying, little Mother, as I write these memories. Does not everything cry out to me to be a saint? [2]

"Then I wrote to my uncle and aunt to acquaint them with my decision. They were absolutely stupe-

---

[1] One could not count on Léonie to replace her because Léonie was herself attracted to the convent.

[2] A short time after her entry into Carmel, Mary wrote to her father: ". . . You give to God all the hope of your old age without counting the cost, and glory is yours! the glory which does not pass. Yes, my beloved father, we will glorify you as you merit to be glorified; we will become saints. Anything else would be unworthy of you."

fied. I, the independent one! I who always had had an air of not being able to stand a convent! I was going to become a religious . . .!

"They could not recover from their astonish-ment."

Chapter Six

In Mary's Garden

"I entered Carmel on October 15th, 1886. While passing under the cloister to go to the choir, I cast a glance at the courtyard. 'It is indeed what I imagined,' I thought. 'How austere it is! Well . . . after all, I didn't come here to see cheerful things.' That was the extent of my enthusiasm!

"In the choir, our venerable Foundress, Mother Genevieve of Saint Therese, was in adoration before the Blessed Sacrament. Her air of peace and holiness struck me forcibly. Then, with you . . . my Pauline of old . . . I was sent to make a tour of the garden. My attraction did not grow. The garden seemed so small to me after the immense enclosure of the Visitation of Mans and, then, everything seemed to me to be so poor. I did not even think of the happiness of being with you, I only thought of wondering how I would pass all my life within those four walls.

"Ah! Mother, I have found Jesus within these four walls and, in finding Him, I have found Heaven. Yes, it is here that I have passed the happiest hours of my life. They have not, however, been free of crosses, because you know how many have been sent to visit us!

"First came the trial of our poor father's illness, that trial which Therese called *our great treasure.*

"Quite often while I was thinking of Papa I asked myself: 'How will his beautiful life end?' I had a secret presentiment that it would end in suffering, but I was far from suspecting what that suffering would be. *

"After it came, however, one day at Mass I saw its value so clearly that I would not have wanted to exchange it for all the treasures of earth.

"And what merit our dear father must have acquired! Indeed, how right he was in saying: 'My children, never fear for me because I am the friend of the Good God.'

"At that time, the story of Job came to my mind. It seemed to me that it was not only his trial but also ours and that Satan, presenting himself again before the Lord, had said to Him: 'It is not surprising that Your servant praises You because You overwhelm him with good things! Strike him then in his own person, and You will see that he will curse Your Name.' But the name of the

---

* Mr. Martin became paralyzed and endured a long illness which affected his mind. [Ed.]

Lord was not cursed. On the contrary it was continually blessed midst the most poignant trials.

"You desire yet, Mother, that I speak to you a little of that distant time when I took my Habit and when I made my Profession. I wonder by what privilege I find myself among these 'Virgins who do not have to seek the dwelling place of the Lord because they themselves walk in His ways.'

"It was especially during the days which followed my reception of the Habit that I best appreciated my good fortune. Every morning, it seemed, I took a Habit *of liberty,* and it was also a feast-day Habit to me. It was all right to say, as in my childhood, *I am free!* . . . Before entering Choir, the only toilette one had to make was a letting down of one's sleeves. My happiness was unbelievable!

"As for my day of Profession, I have no other memory but that it completely resembled the day of my First Communion. My soul was in peace. Jesus had called me and I had come to Him. What happiness can be compared to responding to His voice? He had called me . . . He! Who will ever be able to understand what it means to be called by God? What a mystery! Is He not the Master of His creature? And He invites the creature to love Him . . . He asks if *it wishes* to love Him. But since He is LOVE, He cannot act otherwise,

55

because love must be free. Only, the touching thing is that He desires to be loved and that He appreciates the love of His poor little creature.

"And it is Therese who will crown me! She is like a prelude, an assurance of my eternal crown!

"The evening of my Profession I cried as I had done on the day of my First Communion, *because the second beautiful day of my life had passed.*

"Now, Mother, I want to tell you the impression that Therese made upon me on the day of her entrance into Carmel. I can not say that I experienced a feeling of happiness when I saw her cross the threshold of the cloister. No . . . because I was thinking of our father who was going to be deprived of his treasure . . . But she! What a celestial creature! And how my little Therese had grown! One does not judge such things very well through the parlor grille. Yes, how she had grown and how beautiful she was! The good God had endowed her with all graces. But in Carmel, He permitted that this beauty be veiled, humiliated . . . like a diamond hidden beneath stones. And now He is pleased to make it shine beside His Divine Face before the entire universe, *for ever and ever.*

"Mother, and dearly beloved sister, what more shall I say? Ah! If trials have piled upon us, graces, too, have fallen in torrents.

"The two little doves we had left in the paternal nest, Céline and Therese, flew after us to Carmel. We have seen them at our sides, come to share our life! We have seen Therese die . . . of love! And, not far from us, another sweet dove, Léonie, has found the place of her repose. [1] Tell me if the measure of our consolations has not surpassed that of our sorrows? But our life is not over and more than one suffering awaits us yet. However, why not abandon ourselves to Him Who proportions His grace to the cross, to Him Who has overwhelmed us with so many blessings? I also wish to say to Him like Therese: 'Dear Lord, You overwhelm me with joy in all You do! Does not the cross hide, in fact, eternal joys?' "

---

[1] In 1915 we had the joy of again seeing our sister Léonie, Visitation nun at the Monastery of Caen, under the name Sister Francoise Thérèse. She was called to Lisieux to bear witness before the ecclesiastical tribunal in session at the Carmel. In the notes of Sister Mary of the Sacred Heart we have found the ineffable impression provoked by this meeting.

"We were," she writes, "seated together, all four of us, on the flight of steps near the infirmary. The sky was blue and cloudless. In a moment, time disappeared for me: the time of our childhood, Buissonets, all seemed to me to be a single instant. I saw Léonie a religious, with us! and the past and the present became confused in one unique moment. The past was like a flash; it seemed already to live in an eternal present, and I understood eternity which is entire in a single instant."

Chapter Seven

She Forgot to Mention

But what our dear sister has failed to mention (because she so utterly ignored herself!) is the *virtue* which she always secretly practiced . . . perfume of charity, of goodness, of forgetfulness of herself, and of humility, diffused all about her during fifty-three years of religious life.

She had been "the Angel" of our "little Therese" when Therese entered the convent. Then their communications together became few, and each knew how to lead that cloistered life of detachment, which is never without imposing sacrifices. But even though their talks together became rare, each was well acquainted with the other's state of soul. "Virtue shines naturally," Therese used to say.

"Often," Sister Mary of the Sacred Heart wrote, "in thought, I resaw the time when Therese was among us and I find that nothing can blot out what we have seen. What perfection in everything, and yet, what simplicity! How many times while watching her pass under the cloisters, simple, modest and recollected, I said to myself: 'When I think that

58

here below it will never be known how much this soul loves the good God!' All that one can say and write of her does not give her true portrait. One must have known her. I could not myself describe her, but she is engraved in my soul like a celestial vision which nothing can alter."

And the god-daughter, in turn, wrote to her god-mother during a retreat:

"When I meet you, it seems to me that I am meeting an angel. I see in you what others cannot see, because you know so well how to hide what you are that, on the day of eternity, many will be surprised."

The first duty of Sister Mary of the Sacred Heart in Carmel was to be an aide in the infirmary where, at that time, our venerable Mother Genevieve of Saint Therese lay; she called Mary her *ray of sunshine*. Then, for a time, she worked in the refectory. Finally she became procuratrix, which position she held for forty years—and even longer, because during the years of her infirmity she counselled the acting procuratrix and took charge of our dear Sisters of the White Veil. The latter, moreover, loved her as a Mother and, by her hidden tendernesses she also made herself beloved of all the Community. Her solicitude for the postulants was proverbial. She always obtained permission to suggest to them some practical ways for becoming accustomed to certain rigors of the Rule.

Her office of procuratrix gave her many occasions to practice mortification of her tastes; whatever was least good was enough for her. But it did not go the same for the Community. She would sometimes sigh, saying: "One must not fear to nourish these poor sisters who are always under abstinence." We can still see her passing around the tables, slipping this or that under the napkins of the tired sisters and stealthily tossing a piece of sugar into a bowl of milk.

The following incident will give us an even deeper insight into her supernatural goodness. We have it from one of our Sisters who was then a novice and witnessed an event which surely must have hurt the procuratrix very much. At the time of preparing the portions on the service table, what was her astonishment to see Sister Mary of the Sacred Heart take particular pains with the portion of the nun who had just hurt her. "Why," she exclaimed, "why do you give extra attention to the Sister who offended you? I cannot understand that!" And she received this beautiful answer: "Don't you see, Sister, it is in such simple ways as this that one often restores peace to a heart that suffers. This Sister is good, she is certainly sad at heart, and she is going to be consoled to see that I hold nothing against her."

We must return to the diverse occupations of our humble Sister during her long Carmelite life. With the procuratorship went the care of the garden, from which she cleaned the deep-rooted, perennial couch-grass when a gardener had refused the job. The vegetable garden received her assiduous attention. She also tastefully planted, on all sides, ivy, periwinkle, and roses. While passing in the cloister one day, our dear little Saint smiled at Mary as she was planting a small spruce tree, today a magnificent tree on which a white statue of Therese stands out conspicuously.

The cultivation of the garden and flowers inspired her with this thought:

"A gardener is much pleased when the flowers he has cultivated respond to his care, and when they are rare flowers, his pleasure turns into glory.

"Thus I thought that I was a rare flower, since Jesus had planted me in His chosen garden: Carmel. But, alas! I am *a free flower,* free to give more or less glory to the Divine Gardener. And I have desired to be holy that He may derive more joy in contemplating His flower and that later He may show it to His saints as a marvel of His Grace. I understand, much better than I could ever express it, the disinterested love of the elect. Their own glory is nothing to them; what they wish is merely *to re-count the glory of God.* It is He alone Whom they love; they forget themselves entirely. That is indeed true love because *at the moment one thinks of his own interests, at that moment one ceases to love perfectly.*

"Although I had these beautiful inspirations, it was impossible for me to realize them. I wish also, like Therese, to put all my confidence in Him Who works upon the will and the deed. And I beg my Jesus for this confidence, hoping that my little Therese will obtain for me the ability to say as she did: *'The Lord has taken me and placed me there.'* "

Our gardener mystic . . . may she pardon us this qualification of "mystic", to which she would certainly have objected . . . could continue her prayer each day while busying herself, at a fixed hour, with the baking of altar breads. And we recall with tender edification that, on the very afternoon of Saint Therese's death, Sister Mary, when the saint's agony was beginning, did not ask to be re-placed at her work in the garden.

But we should like to evoke another moving memory, that of July 8th, 1897, when the Saint was taken from her cell to the infirmary. Sister Mary of the Sacred Heart writes:

"I was seated beside her bed. The miraculous statue of the Blessed Virgin had just been placed on a small table against the left wall. Then I read her these lines: 'Thou who didst come to smile on me in the morning of my life . . . come, and smile again, dear Mother, for now the evening is here!'

"Almost instantly her eyes filled with tears as she looked at the Blessed Virgin. I arose and approached, asking if I had caused her any pain. 'No,' she answered, 'but I can not explain to you just now, I would cry . . . ' Finally she confided to me, in tears: *'She never appeared so beautiful!'* 'Are you crying because of consolation?' *'Yes.'* 'And, yet, you are in the dark night of faith?' Making an affirmative gesture, she sighed: 'Ah! Indeed I am!' I was deeply moved; this scene awakened in me so many memories!

"One day in the not too distant past, she had been crying before this very statue, or rather before a real vision of her Heavenly Mother, who had come to cure her. And I was there, alone, at her bedside, ravished by the contemplation of that ecstacy. In Carmel, the good God permitted that I should be there again to see her last tears, and the last smile of Mary to her 'Little Flower.'

" 'It is not like the first time,' she told me, 'Oh! no, it is indeed the statue that I see and which appears so beautiful to me! Formerly, you see, the statue was not placed in the room like that and I only saw it from the side; do you remember? Before, you know well that it was not the statue . . . '

"She did not finish, but I understood, and then said to her: 'It is a consolation for me to have been there alone with you that evening.' 'Oh! that touched me very much,' she answered."

It is to Sister Mary of the Sacred Heart that we owe the Autobiography of Saint Therese because it was she who persuaded us, by her repeated requests, to give Saint Therese the order to write her life, thus being triumphant over our secret (and quite illusory) fear of making her lose her simplicity.

It was she, too, who asked the Little Flower to put "her little doctrine" into writing, for her personal consolation, and received those admirable pages, that sublime resumé of her little way, which make up Chapter XI of her autobiography.

Chapter Eight

Her Sister, Canonized

We must speak to you now, as we have promised, of the feelings of our dear sister with regard to the glorification of our little saint.

From the canonical process, it seems interesting to us to cite the reply that she made to this question: "Why do you desire the Beatification of Sister Therese of the Infant Jesus?"

"I desire it," she explained, "because I think God wills it, and will be glorified by it. He has created us to know Him and to love Him, but few know Him and, consequently, few love Him. He is looked upon as a Judge, a Master; how few regard Him as a Father!

"Sister Therese of the Child Jesus teaches us to go to Him by confidence and love, and when the Church will have sanctioned her way of confidence which does so much good to souls, it seems to me that a greater number of them will come to range themselves under her banner and to follow her example. Because 'God is Love', and it is by love that the creature glorifies Him more.

"Therefore I look upon Sister Therese of the Infant Jesus as an Apostle, the Messenger whom Our Lord has chosen in these latter times to announce to all His Infinite Love for us."

And here are the intimate echoes of her soul, after the great feasts of Beatification, then of Canonization, in 1923 and 1925.

"March 19th, 1924

"Dearly beloved Mother:

"You request my thoughts on the Beatification of our little Therese. Would I be capable of describing them? My soul is so exiled! We have suffered so much for the Cause! However, I cannot say that I did not experience celestial joy during the Triduum in May, last year. How could I forget the feelings I experienced on seeing Cardinal Vico, Prefect of the Congregation of Rites and Legate of the Holy Father, surrounded by his court of honor, and all the prelates and religious gathered in the sanctuary! . . . Yes, my eyes were captivated by this unique glory. It was like a picture of the Judgment. The Church, with her divine majesty, unfolded the judgments of the Lord on our little Therese. There are no words to express what I felt at that moment.

"But, at the same time, trial visited me. You remember, Mother, that I could not kneel because of acute rheumatism that had appeared during the night of the 28th to the 29th of April, on the feast of the Beatification at Rome; besides, my hands were all swollen. But I easily forgot my sufferings before such an event. After so many labors and intimate renouncements, as during the days of deposition at the Process, my little infirmities seemed nothing at all because they were submerged in an ocean of infinite graces.

"Ah! I understand better than ever that there is nothing true, nothing great, nothing noble, but sanctity. Therefore, in all contradictions, let us say like our little Saint: 'Nothing is too much to win the palm!' The good God, in His infinite Goodness, sometimes places us on a battlefield; He wishes to see what we shall do, or rather, He knows well that we are going to confide ourselves to Him and He is ready HIMSELF to fight for us. Poor little combats here below, which will one day so greatly resound in the heavenly kingdom!"

Extract from a second letter:

"The last glorious vision had disappeared, but it has furrowed new abysses in my heart or, rather, it has caused me to ascend ever higher towards the eternal Kingdom! No longer shall we see bishops making their way towards the infirmary to celebrate Mass there.

"No longer shall we see our good Cardinal Vico placing (and with what piety!) the golden rose in the hand of our Therese. The feasts of Canonization have passed; now we await those of Heaven, which will never pass.

"What shall I say to you, my dear little Mother. Ah! I understand that the Blessed Virgin 'kept all these things in Her heart!' One cannot express what one feels on beholding such grandeur responding to a life so hidden.

"During the days which preceded these grandiose feasts, I suffered very much without telling you about it. I wondered how all would go, seeing the bad weather which did not let up and the tempest the evening before which made our decorations fly under the cloisters. Everything might have gone wrong. But the good God did not will it. I prayed so hard to Him in the secrecy of my heart! Oh! how well one knows that there is Someone in our soul Who dwells in its most intimate part. Yes, one feels a Divine Presence . . . one understands that God is in us because when one speaks to Him in the anguish of one's heart, one hears a response of peace.

"However, a certain melancholy sometimes invades us. Why? Is it because we are going towards the unknown, because our earthly life is on the decline, because we tremble to see all that

remains dear to us in this world disappearing?
Yes, it is that indeed! However, we ought to try
to feel just the opposite. What to do? Support
the trial of faith in peace, the trial of death, because it is really towards life that we are moving.
While thinking of death, which so saddens nature,
I suddenly had this inspiration: *It is the day of
great mercy.* What I felt was so profound! I understood that death is the moment when God
overwhelms the soul with a torrent of graces that
He has resolved to give to it from all eternity. It
is the day of His great mercy.

"My little Mother, I love to plunge myself
into this assurance which does me so much good,
because it seems to me that it is the truth.

"You asked me what I thought of the Canonization of our little Sister: for the glory of God
I rejoice at it, but only for His glory, because
Therese has still more power to make Him known
and loved and to draw souls to Him. I think He
has made use of a child to show to the great and
wise ones of the earth the true way to Heaven.
He first made Himself a Child to show us this
way Himself, but we had forgotten it, so He took
up the lesson again by means of our little Therese."

Chapter Nine

More Than Orange Peels

Our very dear Sister, in a third letter which we are about to cite, makes allusion to great sufferings.

The world-reputation of Saint Therese of the Child Jesus drew around her name some writers, amateurs, who pretended to have discovered, in some secret archives, blots of dishonor among the Saint's immediate ancestors.

A manuscript was prepared and, through a shameful bargaining, we, at ,Lisieux, were asked to buy it at a very great price if we did not want to see it published.

Indignant, some friends of the monastery, devout and competent and greatly approved by diocesan authority and even by Rome, did some profound research at the national archives and elsewhere, historically proving the falseness of the odious claims.

Moreover, arbitrarily interpretating some passages of the *Summarium* (Summary of the Process) and certain apocryphal writings, we were accused

70

of having betrayed the truth concerning the character of our Saint.

Here are the sighs of Sister Mary of the Sacred
Heart on this sad subject:

"Saturday, April 10th, 1926
"My little Mother:

"Last Tuesday, when we had just finished'
speaking together of our tribulations and I was
going to Vespers with heavy heart, while entering
the choir I smelt a sweet perfume, especially while
passing the first door, near your stall. I stopped a
moment to try to discover from whence it pro-
ceeded. It was a mingled perfume from several
flowers. On entering the choir I smelt nothing
more, but I understood that our dear little saint
was saying to us: 'I am with you, do not fear anything.'

"It is true, Mother, that we have many sufferings, but I would willingly say with our angelic
Therese: 'I went away fortified by humiliations'.
True grandeur is hidden, because it is a glory to
be associated by suffering to the Passion of Our
Lord; yes, the scorn of the world is a glory. Sometimes I understand that so well! It is when the
good God wills to give us light, the light that dis-
sipates all darkness that hovers over false goods,
false glories of this earth. But I avow that this

71

austere truth is not always so clear to the eyes of my soul.

"The Lord, however, may indeed also rise to defend us. As I opened the Old Testament, this passage from Isaias struck me:

" 'All those who are enflamed against thee will be confounded and covered with shame; thou shalt seek and thou shalt not find those who find fault with thee; they will be like unto nothing, reduced to nothing, those who make war against thee. Because I, Jehovah thy God, will take thee by the right hand. I will say to thee: Fear not, it is I Who come to thine aid.'

"Yes, it is God Who will come to our aid; whatever happens, I will confide myself entirely to Him, even should we be precipitated into the depths of an abyss.

"Our little Therese must be very fearful to Hell, since it organizes so many plots against her! But also, by our sufferings, shall we, too, aid her in saving souls.

"Do not be pained, little Mother. What evil can reach us since we have Our Lord as our Support?"

Our dear Sister, in a letter of March 19th, 1924, spoke of a severe attack of rheumatism that she suffered on the night of Saint Therese's Beatification. Without doubt she was already rheumatic but she was to suffer from this ailment, from that time, more and more.

Until that time, her very good health had permitted her not only to follow the entire Rule but to add even other penances to it.

However, at the end of the year 1924 she was attacked by pneumonia so seriously that we were counselled to have her receive the last Sacraments, but she protested, saying: "No, Mother, believe me, I am not going to die; I have not undergone enough physical pain in Carmel; it will be longer, harder for me."

She wrote to us in 1933:

"Nine years ago, when I was so sick that it was thought to give me Extreme Unction, I said to myself: 'How strange! I am going to die without having suffered; I do not understand this design of God.' And I had a certain regret. Now I see that I was not mistaken and that He loved me too much to deprive me of suffering, because it is the only way in which we can prove our love to Him! Besides I thank Him for it with all my heart."

She recovered very well from the pneumonia, but the rheumatism continued to wrack her with pain. On January 25th, 1929, she had to leave her cell for a little infirmary on the ground floor, furnished as best we could with a little altar opposite the bed, with a beautiful reproduction of the Virgin of the Smile.

Alas! How many renouncements were forced upon her there! She could still walk slowly, on the arm of the charitable infirmarian, but little by little she came to be immobile in an armchair. Her legs and feet swelled and wounds formed on them. How much our dear Sister aroused our compassion! She who was so active . . . how could she support such a trial which prolonged itself eleven years! But she was always serene, despite secret anguish which made her pray without ceasing. She used to say to us:

"Prayer is the state of my soul; I cry night and day to the good God: 'My God, come to my aid! Hasten! Hasten to help me!' And still more to arouse His tenderness: 'Thou Who art my Tender Spouse, have pity on me!' "

Referring to her distress and to the help which she expected from God alone, she confided to us:

"I am capable of all but He, too, is capable of all."

And again:

"I often think of the Blessed Virgin who took pity on the bride and groom at the Marriage Feast

74

of Cana, saying to Our Lord: 'They have no more wine!' And I repeat to Her: 'My good Mother, I too have no more wine! Before, when I was young, I always had the wine of health, knowing neither sickness nor infirmity. But today I have no strength, I have no wine! Ask your divine Son, Who is my Spouse, to have pity on my distress!' "

Then, gathering herself together, she added:

"However, is it indeed true to say that He served the best wine before? No ... It is today, certainly, that He serves me the best: the wine of trial. Thus, as the banquet of my life reaches a close, He has made no mistake ... *He has saved the best wine until now* ... "

Her preoccupation was always to save souls. She groaned, not without heroism:

"I am as though in flames. I feel oppressed, my arms give me great pain, but I offer it to the good God that a soul may not be oppressed and lost for all eternity." We also find this word from her, which well synthesizes her two greatest aspirations: *"Except to love God and to sacrifice oneself to save souls, all is vain."*

"Since our Therese is especially Patroness of Missions, the good God alone knows how ardently I desire to aid her by filling her hands with roses," she said at another time.

And what did our Little Saint do for her big sister, whose eyes so often turned towards the statue which we had placed in a corner by the window . . . the statue of Therese, seated, with the Gospel on her knee. What did she obtain for her dear god-mother, who used to work all day long, assiduously and painfully, with her poor deformed hands, on little reliquaries of her sainted god-child . . . even to the last week of her life!

"I pray to her, and she does not answer me!" she sighed.

However, twice Therese came to her aid visibly.

On February 15, 1939, she wrote to her sister who is a Visitation nun:

". . . It was on January 29, during the night, while I was suffering very much from rheumatism in the knees, and a lay-sister had done all she could to assuage the pain. After many trials, not being able to succeed, she said: 'I am going to pray to our Saint to come to your help.' And she left, full of sadness, but confident.

"Several moments later, I felt as though someone had very gently straightened out my legs, without any effort, and I had no doubt but that it was supernatural intervention. The prayer of my infirmarian had been heard and my little Therese had truly come to my aid. I had absolutely no more suffering the whole night."

Another time, when she was so violently taken with rheumatism in the shoulder that she was unable to make any movement to cover herself, Therese "came down" and, with sisterly hand, placed the covers over the aching member. After thanking her, the god-mother said to her quite simply: "Go back, now, to Heaven."

Chapter Ten

Come, You Will Be Crowned!

On October 15, 1936, we celebrated the Jubilee of our sister's religious profession. She was fifty years a Carmelite.

A large and very beautiful painting, from the brush of one of our Sisters, who was an artist, had been especially prepared. It showed Saint Therese of the Child Jesus, as a postulant, crowning Sister Mary of the Sacred Heart on the day of her profession. In the corner of the picture was His Holiness, Pope Pius XI, giving his blessing to her.

The painting had been sent beforehand to the august Pontiff in the hope that he would write something on it.

What emotion and what joy seized our venerable Jubilarian when the picture was presented to her and, written in the Pontiff's own hand, she read this invitation to the *Eternal* Jubilee: "COME, YOU WILL BE CROWNED!" (Veni Coronaberis).

It was the invitation for which she lived, and longed to answer.

The year following the celebration of her Jubilee was the year of the National Eucharistic Congress at Lisieux, and the blessing of the Basilica . . . the Basilica which she could see from a distance, under the cloister and through the garden, its dome sparkling to the touch of the sun. She often stopped her wheel-chair and gazed with admiration on that *vision of peace,* as she called it.

On July 12 she was taken to the infirmary of our Saint to assist at the Mass celebrated by the Legate of Piux XI, His Eminence, Cardinal Pacelli, and to take Holy Communion from his hand. She had said previously: "I want very much to meet all the Cardinals who come to the Monastery, because it is possible that one day one of them will be Pope, and I would be happy to receive, in Carmel, the blessing of the future Vicar of Christ."

She had been heard.

In the morning, during the visit of the Legate inside the cloister, our venerable Bishop presented Sister Mary to His Eminence, who, approaching her with delicate kindness, smiled paternally upon her, as the Bishop said: "Your Eminence, this is Sister Mary of the Sacred Heart, eldest sister and godmother of Saint Therese of the Child Jesus, to whom we owe the Saint's autobiography."

Two years and a half later, on January 17, 1940, while our sister was dying she was to receive a very special Blessing from the Holy Father, through the intermediary of a Roman Prelate who was a great friend of the Monastery. The day after her death, we received the following telegram:

His Holiness expresses his most heartfelt sympathy in your bereavement and sends to the Community the solace of His Apostolic Benediction.

The Sovereign Pontiff had not forgotten Sister Mary.

And now, what shall we say of those last two years of journey towards the Eternal Jubilee? There was a continual increase of physical sufferings, with always the same sweetness, the same patience, the same flow of graces spreading afar, outside and beyond the Monastery, on souls dear to her . . . the humblest having preference . . . to encourage them, to sustain them with counsel, even to save them. (A great number of letters, thousands of them, came to the Monastery.) Offhand, we remember one person whom Sister Mary, by her maternal solicitude, brought even to religious life; others whom she turned towards conversion, etc. . . . "Do you think that I may be snatching some souls from Hell?" she used often to say to us.

Now . . . about the present war.

The thought of the war and of the evils in its wake was a positive anguish to her. However, as we have already remarked, her desire for the Glory of God came before any other sentiment. *"Ah! provided His reign comes,"* she often repeated, *"all else is but little."*

She loved also to repeat, with feeling of consolation, the words of Saint John of the Cross: *"Do not let yourself be saddened by the troublesome happenings of this world, because then you overlook the benefits they bring and by what secret judgments of God they are disposed for the eternal joy of the elect."*

And here it is well to consider the spirituality which she reflected from Saint Therese.

She was very simple in her piety. Few books found the road of her heart and the genus of her spirit.

One was sent to her, treating of a certain form of union with God that was most complicated.

"But I got rid of it quickly!" she tells us. "It was affirmed in this book: 'If anyone wants to arrive at the state of union, it is absolutely necessary that it beware, with jealous care, not to abandon *for a single instant* the government of its interior *powers* . . . to gather our powers in God is the sole necessity!' And all the while I find, in myself, *no* powers! How would you wish me, dear Mother, to rally my *powers!* Besides I turn to my little Therese; she shows me surely *the way, the truth and the life."*

And this humility charmed the Heart of God, who favored Sister Mary several times with manifestations of His love.

"I was once praying to Therese to prepare me well to receive the good God when I was seized by a feeling of faith so lively and so penetrating that I wondered how I would be able to take one more step towards the Communion grille. If I had seen Our Lord with my eyes, I could not have had more faith. When I had received the Sacred Host, I seemed to hear an interior voice which said: 'Behold thy Creator, thy God, thy Father, and thy Saviour'. But even that does not express what I then experienced. Ah! I knew and felt that I possessed ALL in me."

And again, on November 15, 1914:

"This morning, an hour before rising, I had a little consoling dream. Without seeing Him distinctly, I felt Our Lord near me. He said: 'Your soul is My tabernacle'. I was happy to hear these words, but as I did not want to deceive Him I showed Him a tangled skein from which no threads could be drawn. In my mind this meant: Such is my poor soul! Could it indeed be Your tabernacle!

"But He paid no attention. Then I showed Him the skein saying: 'I understand . . . it is also necessary that Thy Mercy have a chance to act . . .'

And I leaned my head against His Heart, abandoning myself to confidence and to love."

But we will see, now, that our pious Sister had not lost, in Carmel, her original manner of expression. She leaves us this impression of her retreat of May, 1915:

"The good God gave me the same grace that He accorded several months ago. I awoke in the middle of the night with a feeling that someone was loving, in my heart, for me. Then I said: *'I live now not I, but Christ Who liveth in me.'*

"It was a very sweet consolation; but the Good God did not renew it in me because He knows that the life of faith is far better for my soul. I am too lacking in spirituality to have these heavenly consolations. And then, I am always afraid lest the devil be trapping me . . . Therefore, it is better that I remain in the category of blockheads."

Did she not have that beautiful spirit of faith of Saint John of the Cross, who used often to repeat: "My God, increase faith in us!"?

"An ounce of faith," she used to say in turn, "suffices to eradicate all evil."

The night after this, towards morning, Sister Mary had a symbolical dream which she describes to us in these words:

"On top of a mountain, smiling, bathed in sunlight, I saw the Blessed Virgin seated, with a child in front of her which she was protecting with motherly love. It was a beautiful picture, so simple and so sweet! Then I saw a great personage . . . like a venerable monk or prophet, standing and looking on with stupefaction. He had suddenly risen from his solitude to contemplate this beautiful spectacle.

"Immediately I awoke, and I understood that a new era had opened for souls, and that is indeed what the 'little way' is, a mystery of mercy explained by a child. Let no one speak to me of other mysteries! I understand only this one."

Chapter Eleven

Unnoticed Secret

(*Interruption by the Editor*)

It is with misgiving that the narration of Mother Agnes is interrupted here for a word of comment.

Commentaries on "The Little Way" are numerous.

But Mother Agnes herself informed the present writer of an element in "the little way," just mentioned by Sister Mary of the Sacred Heart, which is usually overlooked and, without which, "the little way" is the old, hard way. This element is *affiliation to the Blessed Virgin,* and is particularly ignored in our own country.

It is to be remembered that the sanctity which we admire in Saint Therese and in Sister Mary of the Sacred Heart . . . the simple and direct sanctity seen formerly in an amenable soul and now in an independent one . . . is an outgrowth of the Carmelite vocation, the vocation of *being a special child of Mary.*

And this is not confined to the Carmelite Order.

85

The largest confraternity in the world is the confraternity of the Carmelite Scapular . . . the Confraternity of *special children of Mary.*

On July 16, 1251, the Mother of God stooped to this earth, through the Carmelite Order, and folded the Mystical Body to Her breast with a Sign and Promise: "Receive, my beloved children, this Scapular: Whosoever dies clothed in this shall not suffer eternal fire!"

July 16th is now one of Our Lady's great Feasts . . . the Feast of Her affiliation. In the preface of the Mass of Our Lady of the Scapular, Holy Mother Church sings praise to Her because: "On this day, through the Holy Scapular, She took to Herself special children!"

Today more than two hundred million (200,-000,000) Catholics are affiliated to Our Lady by the Scapular. The Rosary and the Scapular are, as always, the two essential devotions to Our Lady. But the Scapular devotion . . . the devotion of actually being affiliated to Our Lady, being Her "special child" at every moment . . . is given prominence in our day as a *way of spiritual life.*

Jesus and Mary are one. To be united to Mary, therefore, is to be united to Jesus. And it is easy to approach Mary because, howsoever glorified, She is a creature.

The Scapular is such an important devotion

. . . because *it morally unites us to Mary!* And this is the devotion which . . . either in this form instituted by Mary, or in some similar form, such as the wearing of other signs instituted for this purpose . . . *is the real secret of "The Little Way."*

To the American reader, this prominence claimed for the Scapular may seem forced.

Just as one is convinced of the superiority of highly advertised products without cognizance of those little advertised, so the average American Catholic today is liable to look upon several Marian devotions as superior to that basic, Scapular Devotion of *affiliation to Our Lady* . . . sealed by Our Lady with a Promise of Eternal Salvation . . . by a promise to make us saints.

In Europe, the Scapular Devotion holds the primary place among Marian devotions which it has held for centuries. Its excellence is taken for granted. Many Catholics in Italy and Spain would not unconsciously speak or ever pray to Our Lady under any other title than "Our Lady of Mount Carmel" or "Our Lady of the Scapular", so vital is this devotion in spiritual life there. Likewise it has been primary in the lives of the recent saints and in the affection of the Popes.

When death was approaching, Pope Leo XIII . . . author of encyclicals on the Rosary and patron of all devotions to Our Lady . . . called his familiars to his bedside and said: "Let us now make a Novena to Our Lady of the Scapular and I shall be ready to die."

When the Scapular was accidentally removed from the shoulders of Pope Leo X, at the moment of his investiture as Sovereign Pontiff, His Holiness seized the Scapular, exclaiming: "Leave me Mary, lest Mary leave me!" And Pope Benedict XV, celebrated Pontiff of World War I, addressed these words to the seminarians of Rome: "Let all of you have a common language and a common armor, the language, the sentences of the Gospel, the armour, the Scapular of the Virgin of Carmel, which you all ought to wear and which enjoys the singular privilege of protection even after death!"

Our Lady appeared for the last time at Lourdes, in greatest glory, on the Scapular Feast. When the apparition was over, Saint Bernadette wanted to be a Carmelite nun . . . to wear the full Habit of which the Scapular is an abbreviation . . . and when this desire was frustrated because of her illness, she did not care what became of her in life and was apathetic towards any religious vocation. In 1929, when the tomb of St. John don Bosco was opened for ecclesiastical examination, it was found that everything corruptible therein had returned to dust . . . with the single exception of the Saint's brown Scapular! The same wonder occurred in the tomb of that great Marian Saint, Alphonsus Liguouri. Saint Conrad von Altôtten practiced the "Little Way of the Scapular," and used to distribute Scapulars, as porter of a Capuchin Monastery. St. John Vianney, Curé of Ars, after telling a client in the confessional of a miraculous preservation from temptation through the Scapular which had been revealed to him, said: "The Scapular is your Safeguard!" "No other devotion," said Blessed Claude de la Colombière, S. J., "has been confirmed with more numerous, authentic miracles. I would reproach myself were I to weaken your confidence in other devotions to Our Lady, all of which cannot fail to touch Her maternal Heart . . . ; but if Our Lady is propitious to those who practice other devotions, how much *more* propitious must she not be to those who wear Her holy Scapular!"

And one could continue on and on, citing quotation after quotation from Saint and Pope, and example after example of the value of being affiliated to Our Lady by the Scapular. It is only fear of breaking too seriously into Mother Agnes' narrative that prevents the mentioning of further facts which show the nearness of the Scapular Devotion . . . the devotion of affiliation to Our Lady . . . to the Catholic Heart.

But America cannot understand "the little way" until it understands the meaning of affiliation to Our Lady . . . until it becomes more sensible in its set of Marian values. All devotions to Our Lady are *not* of equal value. They are all different vehicles into Our Lady's affection and moral presence, most of them given by Our Lady Herself. The Rosary is a prayer, the wearing of medals and the like are usually gestures of homage, and the wearing of the Scapular is a *state of affiliation to Mary* . . . a contract which bears the reward of Mary's Promise: "Whosoever dies in this shall not suffer eternal fire."

It would be most wasteful for one who prays, or for one who does honor, not to be affiliated. And we can be sure that where there is not affiliation to Our Lady . . . either in the Scapular Devotion, religious vows, consecration, or some other devotion frequently practiced . . . progress in sanctity is hindered by lack of one of its finest aids.

As the present writer explained at length elsewhere (*Mary in Her Scapular Promise,* Chapter 12,) the Little Flower (Saint Therese) had only one secret: the secret of being Mary's child. And many, thinking that her secret stopped at confidence and love, not knowing that the secret of this confidence and love was union with Her Mother of the Scapular, have come to wonder, in their spiritual failures, if Our Lady's "Little Flower of Camel" had not made some mistake in saying that she did nothing which "all little souls" could not imitate.

But her little way was simply that of the Scapular . . . a way in which Mary offers Her Heart to us that we may make it, as it were, our own Heart. St. John Eudes heard Our Lord saying: "I have given you this admirable Heart of My dearest Mother, which is but One with Mine, to be truly your Heart also, in order that the children may have but one Heart with their Mother, and the members have no other Heart but that of their Head, that so you may adore, serve and love God with a Heart worthy of His infinite greatness." And while Therese says: "He thirsts for our ‚Love," Lisieux assures us that Therese "Loved the Blessed Virgin as much as is possible on this earth, and she loved her Holy Scapular, which is Mary's Habit."

This devotion is so simple and so natural to one who practices it, that we would not expect that either Saint Therese, Sister Mary of the Sacred Heart, or anyone else, would find much to say about it.

"The Scapular," says Monsignor Fulton J. Sheen, "bears a double witness: to Mary's protection against the ravages of the flesh occasioned by the Fall, and to Mary's influence as Mediatrix of graces, who covers our souls with the richness of Her Son's Redemption." When we affiliate ourselves to Mary by the Scapular we make sanctity easier for ourselves because we enlist Our Lady's aid. As said previously, when Our Lady came to make the Scapular Promise and to fold the Mystical Body to Her bosom with those powerful words "Shall not suffer eternal fire," She made a gesture towards the fulfillment of Her mission. It is Her mission to give the Incarnate Word to mankind, and She has taken us under Her Mantle where we can easily partake of Her immaculate purity and be worthy, as little children, to receive Her Son.

"This most extraordinary gift of the Scapular," said Pope Pius IX, brings its great usefulness not only to the Carmelite Family of Mary, but also to all the rest of the faithful who wish, affiliated to that Family, to follow Mary with a very special devotion."

This is that single mystery of sanctity, needed today more than ever before, that Sister Mary of the Sacred Heart understood so well.

Chapter Twelve

She Knows!

(Mother Agnes resumes the story)

"*I know* . . . ," Sister Mary of the Sacred Heart wrote. "These two words I address to Jesus . . . *I know* . . . to express my confidence in Him. It does me good to say to Him: "I know" . . . I want thus to make Him understand that *I know* that He reserves for me . . . in my present, poor little trial . . . a happiness that I cannot understand. *I know* . . . Do not explain Your designs, my Jesus: *I know* . . . I have complete confidence in Your love for me. Surely You are happy when I say to You: *I know!* . . ."

We said that Sister Mary had not lost, in Carmel, the originality of her character, an originality always of good alloy, augmented with sallies which not only could not hurt anyone, but which added real charm to her virtue.

Father Dubosq, of unforgetable memory, the Superior of the Seminary of Bayeux and an acquaintance of Sister Mary, knowing her very well from the sessions of the Process of Canonization

93

where he acted officially, wrote to us on August 14, 1922:

"It is tomorrow, I suppose, that you wish a happy feast day to our dear Sister Mary of the Sacred Heart. Tell her that I join with all my heart in your prayers and in all the many congratulations with which she will be surrounded. It is necessary that everyone try to please God *in his own manner,* faithfully using, for that purpose, the type of gifts and of good dispositions which he has received; certainly not everyone in the same way. There is indeed a common basis, which is constituted of obedience to the Rule and to the spirit of the religious and Carmelite vocation, but, on this foundation, everyone should create a pattern according to his own aptitudes, his own Graces; the good God is pleased in these different endeavors. And I say all this to tell you that I pray to Our Lady that She may encourage and sustain our dear Sister Mary of the Sacred Heart in the fervor of the virtues of generous devotion, of joyful forgetfulness of herself, of open, simple service to her neighbor and to the good God which are, I believe, her *form of Grace.* This is without forgetting the brusque sallies of her delightful originality, which agreeably season all the good she does."

This portrait could not be more faithful. However, even more do we prefer this other, softer portrait, drawn by her Sainted sister, twenty-eight years before:

THE PORTRAIT OF A SOUL I LOVE

M I *know* Mary. She is my loving sister

A who received, from above, a sublime faith.

R Nothing, no, nothing in this poor exile satisfies her;

I she needs the good God, her only Master and her King.

E And He has made her an ardent and generous queen,

d at once sweet and alive, always humble of heart.

u A distant horizon, a luminous star,

S often suffice to unite her to her Lord.

A Formerly I saw her in her independence,

C seeking true happiness in full liberty;

R to diffuse benefits was her joy

E and to forget herself, for all, her only pleasure.

C It was the Divine Spouse Who captured this soul,

Œ masterpiece of His love, worthy of the Creator;

U one day I shall see her, like a pure flame,

R shining in Heaven beside the Sacred Heart.*

---

* In the French, original version, this is a poem, each line beginning with a letter of Sister Mary's name, technically known as an acrostic. [Ed.]

Our good father used to call his eldest daughter *his diamond,* which is another striking portrait. How many different facets there were to this beautiful diamond of so pure a water! We have revealed several in these pages, except *"that which was hidden within"* and shone for Jesus alone . . .

And now it remains to speak of the last sickness and death of our virtuous sister. And first of the great sacrifice demanded of her on November 27, 1939, six weeks before this precious death. The lay-sister who had cared for her and tenderly loved her, being totally devoted to her charge, day and night, for eight years, was suddenly taken to a hospital for an urgent and unexpected operation.

We could never describe the expression on the face of our venerable sister at the moment of separation . . . an expression of repressed sadness and silent resignation; she thought she would never again see her dear little infirmarian, who was returned to her, fifteen days before her death, and united her suffering to that of Our Lord in the Garden of Olives, offering it to Him for the salvation of souls.

Our merit-accruing invalid coughed frequently during several months, having, as we thought, taken cold. This state, which somewhat disturbed us, developed into pulmonary congestion, at first slight, then grave. On Monday, January 16, we still had

some hope. But on Tuesday morning, no further
illusion was possible and, in the afternoon, placed
in her wheel-chair, she received the Sacrament of
Extreme Unction and the Indulgence *in articulo
mortis.*

Then the chaplain, upon our invitation, approached to give her a word of encouragement, and
received a glance, a smile, a word, that will never
be effaced from his memory. He had heard her
confession for the last time on Wednesday of the
week preceding, and we knew, from herself, to
what point . . . displeased with herself . . . she had
humiliated herself by saying she was the most im-
perfect of creatures. When we spoke of this to the
chaplain, he answered: "Ah! the dear god-mother!
It is always thus with her . . . " And then, without hesitation, he added, "It is she who directs
me!"

This good priest had recently spoken the following words to her, which gave her great comfort:
"Do not fear, your lamp is so well lighted!"

On Wednesday and Thursday, he brought her
Holy Communion. On the latter day, January 18,
she rallied for a few hours in the afternoon; but
she seemed absorbed and no longer spoke. Once,
however, she gave me a long glance and said, with
deep tenderness: *"My dear Mother!"*

A moment later she added: "I haven't a shadow of courage!"

I answered: "However, you are very near Heaven and I believe that you will enter without the slightest deviation." She sighed: "Oh! how much I desire that!"

"Do you fear death?" I asked.

"Not at all," she murmured.

On this last afternoon, great joy was given her by the reading of a letter signed by His Holiness, Pope Pius XII, who deigned to bless the Community and charged me to transmit a paternal message to some particularly dear souls . . . precisely those for whom our venerable invalid had so much prayed and suffered.

Struggling from a half-sleep, she murmured with emotion: "Oh! how good the Holy Father is! How much he is concerned for souls!"

Although we put her back in bed with almost unspeakable difficulty, we spoke to her of the merits which, by her sufferings, she would still be able to acquire for the conversion of sinners in these last hours of her trial: *"Oh! yes,"* she answered in a dying voice, *"souls! souls! . . . There are so many who do not love the good God! Oh! how sad it is!"*

This exclamation puts us in mind of another cry which escaped from her heart previously: "Ah!

how is it possible not to love a God so powerful, so great, so good, Who does all for our well-being. If I went to hell, I would say to Him during all Eternity: *"My God, I love you!"*

In the evening, we assured her that our little sainted sister was present at her side, to aid her unto the end. She could not answer except by a sign, which said: "Yes, I am sure of it."

After Matins we had the Community come; she smiled at all the sisters with so good and so sweet a smile! She did not seem crushed, but rather to the contrary. Her firm attitude seemed rather to reveal the sentiments of a warrior who valiantly enters a decisive battle. Just as we were saying that she no longer had strength enough to hold her crucifix, which was lying before her on the blanket, she immediately put forth her hand, seized it and kissed it with fervor, saying: *"I love you!"*

That was her last intelligible word. Then most of the Sisters left, having been assured that they would be called at the last moments, which came, much sooner than we expected, at two o'clock in the morning.

A little before this last moment, our good Sister made a little sign of farewell to a lay Sister who was standing on the side of the bed towards which her head was inclined.*

A few seconds later, she closed her eyes and began a rather long prayer. She articulated, but without sound. We did not catch the words, but the infirmarian, having gotten very close to the bed, thought she distinguished these words of the "Our Father": *"Thy Kingdom come! . . . "* And, her prayer continuing, we thought that she was reciting the "Hail Mary," followed by the Act of Consecration to God's Merciful Love, which was so fitting at that last hour . . . *"And my soul flies without delay into the eternal embrace of Thy merciful Love."*

When she became silent, suddenly straightening her head, she opened her eyes wide. They were full of light and assurance. She fixed them upwards, then turned them and held them in a long gaze on the statue of the Virgin of the Smile. Then,

---

* This Sister had always been very devoted to her; she was strong, and had put her to bed every night for a long while, and she had never left without making this sign of the hand which resembled the beating of wings, then she would point her finger Heavenwards and say: "You are not going there alone!" This always encouraged Sister Mary of the Sacred Heart, who was so desirous of saving souls. One day, even, she said: "Oh! how much I should like to hear it again!" And immediately the little Sister answered: "You do not go to Heaven alone!"

she inclined her head and expired, with a face so peaceful and so happy that, gazing upon it, we remained consoled and, with this impression, recited the *Subvenite*.

The Community was going to have a genuine disappointment, on awaking, not to have been present as we had promised they would be. Nevertheless, they were called, not in the usual manner but in the manner used on the great days of the Beatification and Canonization of Saint Therese: the joyful pealing of little bells, suspended from an iron ring.

"That heavenly call will always remain engraved in our memory," the Sisters said. Much moved, they all ran to kneel and to contemplate with rapture the rejuvenated face, so sweet and so abandoned, of the one who had left the earth.

After the ringing of the *Angelus* at six o'clock in the morning, Sister Genevieve of the Holy Face was gazing sadly at the statue of our little Saint when she was favored with a sweet and strong odor of incense, very penetrating, which consoled her.

Later, two Sisters also smelled mysterious perfumes; the one . . . Mother Sub-Prioress . . . while praying at the tomb; the other . . . the lay Sister of whom we just spoke . . . while in the laundry, washing the linen of the one who had so long edi-

fied her by her patience and her desire *not to go
to Heaven alone.*

And we think that our Saint Therese, as gift
of joyous welcome, doubtlessly obtained from the
good God for a time that *"the roses belong to
Mary!"*

It remains for us to confide that, during Sister Mary's agony, I had asked her in a very low
voice: "Did you write to me, as you do each year,
the traditional little letter for my feast of Saint
Agnes?" And she let me understand that she had.

Several hours later, alone beside our blessed
Sister, as she rested in her last sleep, I opened the
little envelope which I easily found after her death.
Not without shedding sweet tears, I read that last
letter, dated in advance for January 21, 1940:

"My dear little Mother:

"You have asked me to write for you, for
your Feast, a passage of the Gospel that has been
a light to me, because I often wondered: 'Whatever shall we do in Heaven, during all Eternity?'
These words of Our Lord suddenly came to my
mind: 'Eternal life consists in knowing Thee,
Thee and Him Whom Thou has sent.' There is
not too much eternity for knowing the infinite
goodness of the good God, His infinite power,
His infinite mercy, His infinite love for us. Be-

hold, these are our eternal delights which will know no satiety; our hearts are made to understand them and to be nourished by them.

"Often, before going to Holy Communion, I love to say the act of contrition: 'My God, I am heartily sorry for having offended Thee because Thou art infinitely good and deserving of all love, and because sin displeases Thee . . . ' It is not because I fear a reproach, or Thy chastisements, but because Thou art infinitely good, infinitely perfect and, through love, I ought always to seek to please Thee; this ought to be my only object, my sole bliss.

"Here below, I understand what Thou art, a little, but in life eternal, when I shall see Thee face to face, I shall have a clearer knowledge of Thee, my God, Who art my Creator and my Father and Who hast given me such great proofs of Thy love. Formerly, my little Mother, I liked to think that in Heaven I would know all the marvels of nature, all the beauty of the stars, and their immensity. Now, all that interests me but little and I desire but one thing; to lose myself in Him Who hast created so many marvels . . .

"Happy feast day to my dear Mother, of whom I am always happy sister and child.

Sr. Mary of the Sacred Heart, c. d. i."

Today, she whom the Community is pleased to call "The *incomparable* Sister and God-mother of Saint Therese of the Child Jesus, reposes under the shrine of her glorious god-child, in a vault which has an opening inside the Monastery, very near the choir where, every day, we sing the praises of Him Whom this soul loved ceaselessly with the most generous love. She sees now, for herself and for souls, the reward of her confidence in trial.

She knows.

Chapter Thirteen

"If I Meet You, Friend"

So this letter from Lisieux was just a letter about orange-peel sacrifices . . . about the sanctity of turning off a radio program, picking up a piece of wastepaper, staying home from a Class B movie . . . the sanctity of Saint Therese of Lisieux, whose statue is to be found in practically every Catholic church in the world, although she is dead less than fifty years.

It is a message addressed to us as we are living through the world's greatest trial, its most universal and painful war, and not written with high-sounding words, but in the simple life and heart of a Carmelite nun.

The thought of the war was a positive anguish to her.

But she immediately raised her heart to God, thinking only of His glory and of His values . . . which are eternal.

Whether we save, or gain the entire world, Our Lord would say to us again today: "What does it profit a man, . . . if he suffer the loss of his own soul?"

Do we have to fear the hatred of Anti-Christians from without, so much as lack of Christian love from within?

Often, in times like these, an indescribable feeling of abandon comes over us, as was particularly noticeable in Austria, just before the blitz, when whole congregations sat restless through Sunday Mass and sermon . . . when stones flew through windows of pacifists and waves of pornographic literature rolled from the newsstands. Fear . . . fear not only of physical attack but also of social and economic insecurity . . . very often causes a restlessness that leads to the loss of that which is worth more than the whole world.

The "safety" is CONFIDENCE in God, a clinging to the values of Faith, as *children of Mary*.

Coming from Lisieux, as though no tanks were thundering along the roads of Holland, no dive bombers were razing Amsterdam to dust, no motorized units were soon to be roaring towards Lisieux itself . . . this sweet, peaceful letter, about a girl who began to live when she gave away an orange-peel, is a message that should give us light and courage.

"My soul was in peace" . . . that was the only recollection Sister Mary of the Sacred Heart re-

106

tained of the zenith day of her life . . . the day of her religious profession.

Perhaps that is the thing to remember about Sister Mary of the Sacred Heart herself . . . or, for that matter, about *happiness*.

In the disruption of external peace we may not be able to carry on life as usual, but we must keep our hearts turned to God *more* than usual. We should say more often "My God, I love Thee! I trust Thee! I know this world is passing and I shall live for Thee alone!"

In 1942, writing to make a donation for providing Catholic soldiers with the Carmelite Scapular (because of the promise "Whosoever dies in this shall not suffer eternal fire") a woman in Pittsburgh said: "War is not new to me. I have a brother buried in France; my husband, dead eight years, was a crippled veteran of World War I. To make this donation is a great sacrifice for me because I have little income and I am ill. But," and here she practically echoed the words that are essential in the message of Sister Mary of the Sacred Heart, "I know that nothing is more important than assuring the salvation of souls."

If any of us catch a little of this courage from the life of Sister Mary, a little of her self-sacrifice and love for God, then the letter from Lisieux will not have been written in vain.

Yes, in these troublous times, if I were walking along the street or a country road, or were in a railway station or subway train, and met *you,* I would point my thumb Heavenward in the familiar Victory gesture and say: "Souls up! *Remember the letter from Lisieux!"*

If we do remember this letter from Lisieux and follow its simple message of sanctity, victory shall be ours . . . someday . . . we, too, shall know.

Appendix

Some of the revealing letters written by

Saint Therese

to Sister Mary of the Sacred Heart

NOTE: Out of these letters, and with the help of the Autobiography of Saint Therese, it would have been
possible to turn the letter from Lisieux, just delivered to the reader, into a mighty story.

It has been the editor's object, however, to forsake
the opportunity of telling a mighty story that he
might be the bearer of an even mightier message
for, in the letter from Lisieux, he feels that a
message of perseverance in "the little way" is being
deliberately delivered by Divine Providence over
bloody battle-fields, ruined cities.

But the reader can, from these letters, catch a little
of the drama of those two beautiful lives . . . of
the godchild who preceded, and of the godmother
who followed. If we all follow, then certainly, as
was said . . . we all shall know . . . we all shall
obtain "free entrance into His kingdom."

Letters to Sister Mary of the Sacred Heart

I

February 21, 1888.

DEAREST MARY,—You cannot think what a lovely present Papa made me last week; I believe if I gave you a hundred or even a thousand guesses you would never find out what it was. Well, he bought me a new-born lamb, all white and fleecy. He said that before I entered Carmel he wanted me to have this pleasure. We were all delighted, especially Céline. What touched me more than anything was Papa's thoughtfulness. Besides, a lamb is symbolical, and it made me think of Pauline.

So far, so good, but now for the sequel. We were already building castles in the air, and expecting that in two or three days the lamb would be frisking around us. But the pretty creature died that same afternoon. Poor little thing, scarcely was it born when it took ill and died. It looked so gentle and innocent that Céline made a sketch of it; then we

111

laid it in a grave dug by Papa. It appeared to be asleep. I did not want the earth to be its covering, so we put snow upon our pet, and that was the end.

You do not know, dearest godmother, how this little creature's death has made me reflect. Clearly we must not become attached to anything, no matter how innocent, because it will slip from our grasp when we least expect it; nothing but the eternal can content us.

II

(Written during her retreat before receiving the Habit.)

January 8, 1889.

Your little *lamb*—as you love to call me, dearest sister—wishes to borrow from you a little courage. I cannot speak to Our Lord, and He is silent too. Pray that my retreat may be pleasing to the Heart of Him who alone reads the secrets of the soul.

Life is full of sacrifice, it is true, but why seek happiness here? For life is but "a night to be spent in a wretched inn," as our holy Mother St. Teresa says. I assure you my heart thirsts ardently for happiness, but I see clearly that creatures cannot quench that thirst. On the contrary, the oftener I should drink from their tempting waters the more burning would my thirst become. I know a source where *"they that drink shall yet thirst,"*[1] but with a delicious thirst, a thirst one can always allay. . . . That source is the suffering of which Jesus alone is aware.

III

August 14, 1889.

You ask for a word from your little *lamb*. But what shall I say? Is it not you who have taught me? Remember those days when I sat upon your knee, and you talked to me of Paradise.

I can still hear you saying: "Look at those who want to become rich, and see how they toil for gold. Now, little Therese, with far less trouble and at any hour of the day, we can lay up riches in the Kingdom of God. Heavenly diamonds are so plentiful that we can gather them, so to speak, with a garden rake, and we do this by performing all our actions for the love of God." Then I would leave you, my heart overflowing with joy, and fully bent on amassing great wealth.

Time has flown since those happy hours spent together in our dear nest. Jesus has visited us, and has found us worthy to be tried in the crucible of suffer-

113

ing. God has said that on the last day *"He will wipe away all tears from our eyes,"*[2] and no doubt the more tears there are to dry, the greater will be the happiness.

Pray tomorrow for the little one who owes you her upbringing, and who, without you, might never have reached Carmel.

IV

(During her retreat before profession.)

September 4, 1890.

The heavenly music falls but faintly on the ear of your child, and it has been a dreary journey towards her bridal day. It is true her Betrothed has led her through fertile lands and gorgeous scenery, but the dark night has prevented her admiring, much less revelling in, the beauty all around. Perhaps you think this grieves her. Oh no! she is happy to follow her Betrothed for His own sake, and not for the sake of His gifts. He is so ravishingly beautiful, even when He is silent—even when He hides from us. Weary of earthly consolation, your little child wishes for her Beloved alone. I believe that the work of Jesus during this retreat has been to detach me from everything but Himself. My only comfort is the exceeding strength and peace that is mine. I hope to be just what He wills I should be, and in this lies all my happiness.

Did you but know how great is my joy at giving pleasure to Jesus through being utterly deprived of all joy! . . . This is the very refinement of joy— the joy we do not even feel.

V

September 7, 1890.

Tomorrow I shall be the Spouse of Jesus, of Him whose *"look was as it were hidden and despised."*[3] What a future is opened up! How can I thank Him, how render myself less unworthy of so great a favour?

I thirst after Heaven, that blessed abode where our love for Jesus will be without bounds. True, we must pass through suffering and tears to reach that home, but I wish to suffer all that my Beloved is pleased to send me; I wish to let Him do as He wills with His "little ball." You tell me, dearest god-mother, that my Holy Child[4] is beautifully adorned for my wedding-day, but that you wonder why I have not put new rose-coloured candles. The old ones appeal to me more because they were lighted

115

for the first time on my clothing-day. That day they were fresh and beautiful. Papa, who had given them, was there, and all was gladness. But now their tint has faded. Are there yet any rose-coloured joys on earth for your little Thérèse? No, for her there remain only the joys of Heaven . . . Heaven, where the hollowness of all created things gives place to the uncreated Reality.

VI

MY DEAREST SISTER,— . . . How can you ask me if it be possible for you to love God as I love Him! My desire for martyrdom is as nothing; it is not to such desires I owe the boundless confidence that fills my heart. They might be described as spiritual riches, which are *the mammon of iniquity*,[5] when one takes delight in them as in something great. . . . These aspirations are a consolation Jesus sometimes grants to weak souls like mine—and there are many such! But when He withholds this consolation, it is a special grace. Remember these words of a holy monk: "The martyrs suffered with joy, and the King of Martyrs in sorrow." Did not Jesus cry out, *"My Father, remove this chalice from Me"*?[6] Do not think, then, that my desires are a proof of my love. Indeed I know well that it is certainly not

116

because of them that God takes pleasure in my soul. What does please Him is to find me love my littleness, my poverty, and to see the blind trust which I have in His mercy. . . . That is my sole treasure, dearest godmother, and why should it not be yours?

Are you not ready to suffer all that God wills? Assuredly; and so if you wish to know joy and to love suffering, you are really seeking your own consolation, because once we love, all suffering disappears. In truth, if we were to go together to martyrdom, you would gain great merit, and I should have none, unless it pleased Our Lord to change my dispositions.

Dear sister, you who love Jesus and long to be his little victim, do you not understand that the more weak and wretched we are, the better material do we make for His consuming and transfiguring fire? . . . The simple desire to be a victim suffices, but we must also consent to remain always poor and helpless, and here lies the difficulty: "Where shall we find one that is truly poor in spirit? We must seek him afar off," says the author of the *Imitation*.[7] He does not say that we must search among great souls, but "afar off"—that is to say, in abasement and in nothingness. Let us remain far from all that dazzles, loving our littleness, and content to have no joy. Then we shall be truly poor in spirit, and Jesus will come to seek us, however far off we may be, and transform us into flames of love. . . . I long to make you understand what I feel. Confidence alone must lead us to love. . . . Does not fear lead to the thought of the strict justice that is threatened to sinners? But that is not the justice Jesus will show to such as love Him.

God would not vouchsafe you the desire to be the victim of His merciful love, were this not a favour in store—or rather already granted, since you are wholly surrendered unto Him and long to be consumed by Him, and God never inspires a longing which He cannot fulfill.

The road lies clear, and perforce do we run along it together. I feel that Jesus wishes to bestow on us the same graces; He wishes to grant us both a free entrance into His Kingdom. Dearest godmother, you would like to hear more of the secrets which Jesus confides to your child, but human speech cannot tell what the human heart itself can scarcely conceive. *Besides, Jesus confides His secrets to you likewise. This I know, for you it was who taught me to listen to His divine teaching.* On the day of my Baptism you promised in my name that I would serve Him alone. You were the angel who led me and guided me in my days of exile and offered me to Our Lord, so that I love you even as a child loves its mother, and *not until we pass through the gates of Heaven will you realise the gratitude with which my heart is full to overflowing.*

Your little daughter,

THERESE OF THE CHILD JESUS.

1 Ecclus. xxiv. 29.
2 Apoc. xxi. 4.
3 Isa. liii. 3.
4 An allusion to the statue of the Holy Child in the cloister, which was under the Little Flower's care. (Ed.)

5 Luke xvi. 2.
6 Luke xxii. 42.
7 Cf. Imit. II., ch. xi. 4.